Primary Concepts

Word Problem of the Day

Joan Westley and Kelly Stewart

Cover illustration: Gavid Muradov, Age 9
Baku, Azerbaijan
© River of Words

Designer: Candace Wesen

©2008 Primary Concepts
P.O. Box 10043
Berkeley, CA 94709
www.primaryconcepts.com

All rights reserved.
Printed in the U.S.A.

No part of this book may be reproduced, stored in a retrieval system
or transmitted in any form or by any means, electronic, mechanical, photocopying,
recording, or otherwise, without the prior written
permission of the publisher.

ISBN 978-1-60184-127-8

Contents

Teaching Notes v
Word Problems
   Mother's Day Picture It 1
   The Penny Jar Show It 2
   A New Friend Do It 3
   Planning a Party Use Symbols 4
   Mr. Wordly Cleans House Make a List .5
   A Fear of Heights Picture It 6
   Line Dancing Act It Out 7
Performance Assessment 8
   The Birthday Party Use Symbols 9
   The Biggest Cat Picture It 10
   The Ice Cream Truck Act It Out 11
   Three Balls Use Symbols 12
   Who Set the Table? Do It 13
   An Amazing Sight Picture It 14
   More Pennies in the Jar Show It 15
Performance Assessment 16
   Home Sweet Home Make a List 17
   Shapes in a Rug Picture It 18
   Forming Teams Act It Out 19
   Uncle Nate's Farm Use Symbols 20
   The Last Appointment Make a List . .21
   Sharing Cookies Show It 22
   Collecting Rocks Picture It 23
Performance Assessment 24
   Dad's Trip Do It 25
   Kickball Picture It 26
   The Photograph Use Symbols 27
   Pocket Change Show It 28

   Dance Steps Act It Out 29
   The Petting Zoo Make a List 30
   Cake for Mom Make a List 31
Performance Assessment 32
   Fruit for Lunch Picture It 33
   The Soccer Team Act It Out 34
   A Crate for Lulu Show It 35
   A Picky Eater Use Symbols 36
   Squares in a Quilt Make a Model 37
   Doctor's Appointment Make a List . . .38
   Pieces on a Game Board Picture It . .39
Performance Assessment 40
   Stuffed Animals Picture It 41
   The Overdue Book Do It 42
   Pajama Drawer Picture It 43
   Lulu and the Cat Toys Show It 44
   Birthday Balloons Picture It 45
   Worm Tally Use Symbols 46
   The Orange Cat Show It 47
Performance Assessment 48
   Hungry for Pizza Picture It 49
   The Field Trip Show It 50
   Bagels for the Team Use Symbols 51
   Fish for the Aquarium Picture It 52
   The Necklace Find a Pattern 53
   Cold and Colder Do It 54
   Lines at the Movie Act It Out 55
Performance Assessment 56

Lucky Day Show It 57	**Magazine Subscriptions** Show It . . .73
Eggs for Breakfast Picture It 58	**The Party of 14** Picture It 74
Wheel Count Use Symbols 59	**Coins in the Couch** Show It 75
Buttons on a Dress Find a Pattern . . .60	**Game Time** Make a List 76
Fruit Juice for Friends Use Symbols . .61	**Treats on a Hot Day** Use Symbols 77
Wedding Shoes Make a List 62	**Making Lunches** Make a List 78
A Package of Pencils Show It 63	**Penny Trading** Show It 79
Performance Assessment 64	**Performance Assessment** 80
The Garden Show It 65	**Picture Day** Show It 81
Visiting Uncle Nate Do It 66	**Stepping Stones** Make a Model 82
Jumping Contest Act It Out 67	**Money in the Bank** Show It 83
The Striped Rug Find a Pattern 68	**The Neighbor's Address** Find a Pattern 84
Shoes at the Door Picture It 69	**Buying a Cat Door** Use Symbols 85
Sausages and Buns Use Symbols 70	**A Gift for Grandma** Make a Model . . .86
The Heaviest Pumpkin Use Symbols .71	**Waitress Outfits** Picture It 87
Performance Assessment 72	**Performance Assessment** 88
	Vocabulary Index 89
	Strategies Index 90

Word Problem of the Day

Word problems are a terrific way to build comprehension skills. Teachers have long recognized that when children solve word problems, their biggest stumbling block is often not the math computation but understanding the problem. Learning to understand problems should begin early, as young as kindergarten.

Word Problem of the Day is a unique approach to problem solving because it presents problems that focus on language skills rather than on math skills. The problems follow the typical word problem format, but children need only the most rudimentary math skills to solve them. Unlike many word problems in math texts, children must really listen to the wording of these problems in order to solve them. Simply taking the numbers and performing the operation that they are studying is not sufficient. The focus is exclusively on making meaning from the story. Children must pay careful attention to details, visualize the situation, and solve the problem.

Getting Started

Beginning with the first word problem, introduce a problem a day to your class. All the word problems in the book involve the Wordly family, just an ordinary family that faces ordinary problems that have ordinary solutions. (If you have been using the vocabulary-building series *Word of the Day,* your students are already acquainted with the Wordlys.)

Use questions like those in the Talk About It section to help children understand the problem and relate it to their personal lives and prior knowledge. Clarify any vocabulary words that children are having difficulty understanding. Commonly misunderstood words are italicized. Reread the word problem as necessary.

Then introduce the strategy for solving the problem. The *Word Problem of the Day* strategies, which are listed on the next page, will prove useful for all kinds of comprehension situations. The emphasis is on visualizing the story and making the situation come alive for the children. Again, you will need to reread the word problem as children use the strategy to solve the problem. On page 90, you will find a list of the pages where each strategy occurs.

Act It Out   Do It
Find a Pattern   Make a List
Make a Model   Picture It
Show It   Use Symbols

After children have settled on a solution, reread the problem one last time, rewording it as necessary and connecting the answer back to the problem.

Extending the Learning

Every once in a while, put the book aside and invite the children to make up their own problems. Have the children present their problems to the class to solve. Use the children's problems for the Word Problem of the Day rather than the ones in this book.

Performance Assessment

Scattered throughout the sequence of lessons are performance assessment opportunities. Performance Assessment problems give teachers the chance to monitor how well individual children are progressing. Are they able to solve problems on their own? The problems chosen for Performance Assessment do not involve new vocabulary, and children can solve them in many different ways.

Introduce these word problems in the same way as you do the others, but let the children pick their own problem solving strategies. Have students show their thinking with pictures and words.

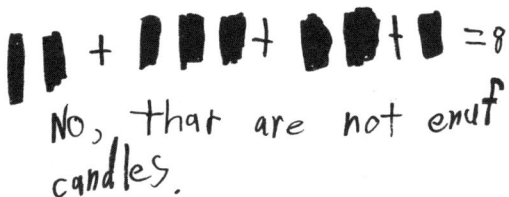

Mother's Day

Word Problem

The Wordly children want to make a colorful bouquet for Mother's Day. They pick a red flower. They pick two yellow flowers. They pick a purple flower. They can't find any orange flowers to pick. For green, they find a leaf.

How many flowers do they pick?

Talk About It

- What is a bouquet?
- Do the children pick an orange flower? Do they pick a green flower?
- Are we trying to figure out how many different colors the children use in the colorful bouquet? What question are we trying to answer?

Picture It   *Materials: paper and crayons or markers*

Draw a picture of the bouquet. Count the flowers.

Solution

The Wordly children pick four flowers in all (one red flower, two yellow flowers, and one purple flower).

The Penny Jar

Word Problem

The Wordlys decided to keep a *penny* jar. When the jar was full, they would give the money to charity. On the first day, the oldest Wordly boy put in three pennies. Mrs. Wordly put in two pennies. Mr. Wordly had only one penny to put in the jar. No one else had any pennies.

How many pennies were in the penny jar at the end of the first day?

Talk About It

- Why did the Wordlys have a penny jar?
- Are we trying to find out how many pennies the Wordlys will give to charity? What are we trying to find out?

Show It   *Materials: counters or pennies*

Use counters to show the pennies. Count out three pennies, then two pennies, then one penny. Then count the total.

Solution

There were six pennies in the penny jar at the end of the first day.

A New Friend

Word Problem

A new friend of one of the Wordly boys came over after school one day. Mrs. Wordly introduced herself and asked him his name. He said, "My name has three letters. The *last* letter is *M*. The *first* letter is the *third* letter in the alphabet. The *second* letter is the first letter in the alphabet." Mrs. Wordly said, "I'll have to write that down!"

What is the boy's name?

Talk About It

- How many letters are in the boy's name? (three)
- What is the first letter of the alphabet? second? third?

Do It   *Materials: paper and pencil*

Write the letters of the boy's name.

Solution

The first letter is *C*, the second letter is *A*, and the third letter is *M*. His name is Cam.

Planning a Party

Word Problem

The Wordlys were planning a party. Mrs. Wordly said, "We must invite Grandma Wordly, of course. Uncle Jim can bring her. Let's invite the *twins*, too." Mr. Wordly thought about it and said, "I think that's *too many* people. We have only four extra chairs."

Are there *enough* chairs?

Talk About It

- How can we figure out how many guests Mrs. Wordly is inviting?
- Mrs. Wordly wants to invite the twins. How many is that?
- How many people would be too many? Why?
- Could there be more than enough chairs? What does *more than enough* mean?

Use Symbols   *Materials: paper and pencil*

Draw a square to represent each chair. On each chair, mark an X for each guest.

Solution

There are enough chairs. Four guests are coming, and there are four extra chairs.

Mr. Wordly Cleans House

Word Problem

Mr. Wordly was cleaning the house. *First*, he cleaned the living room. *Next*, he cleaned his office. *After* that, he cleaned the bathroom. Then he decided to have lunch in the kitchen. When Mrs. Wordly came home, Mr. Wordly told her he had made a lot of progress.

How many rooms had Mr. Wordly cleaned?

Talk About It

- How can we keep track of how many rooms Mr. Wordly cleaned?
- Why did he stop? (for lunch)
- Did Mr. Wordly clean the kitchen? (no)

Make a List   *Materials: paper and pencil*

Make a list of each room Mr. Wordly cleaned. Count the number of rooms.

Solution

Mr. Wordly cleaned three rooms (living room, office, and bathroom).

A Fear of Heights

Word Problem

Mrs. Wordly is afraid of heights. She doesn't like to climb ladders, but one day she decided to try. The ladder she used had only five steps. When she got to the *third* step, she said to herself, "I think I'm *halfway* there."

Is Mrs. Wordly right?

Talk About It

- What is Mrs. Wordly afraid of?
- What does *halfway there* mean?
- If she is halfway to the top, can there be *more* steps *above* her than *below* her?

Picture It   *Materials: paper and pencil*

Draw a ladder with five steps. Mark the step that Mrs. Wordly is on. How many steps are above her? How many steps are below her?

Solution

Yes, Mrs. Wordly is halfway to the top.

Line Dancing

Word Problem

One of the Wordly girls is learning how to line dance. In line dancing, the boys and girls need to *pair* up. At one line dancing class, there were seven girls and five boys.

How many *more* girls than boys were there?

Talk About It

- Are we trying to find out how many boys and girls there were in all? What is the question?
- If there were the *same* number of girls as boys, how many girls would there be? (five)

Act It Out

Let's count out boys and girls to represent the children in the class. These children can stand in front of the classroom and pair up for line dancing. How many pairs are there? How many girls are left?

Solution

There were two more girls than boys.

Performance Assessment

Word Problem

The youngest Wordly girl collects small, bouncy balls. She keeps her balls in an old peanut butter jar. So far, she has two blue, one red, three green, and two yellow balls. She really wants a glow-in-the dark ball!

How many bouncy balls does the Wordly girl have?

Talk About It

- What does the Wordly girl collect? Do you collect anything?
- Does she have a glow-in-the dark ball?
- Are we trying to find how many different colors of balls the Wordly girl has? What is the question?

Solve It   *Materials: paper and crayons or markers*

Use pictures and words to show your answer.

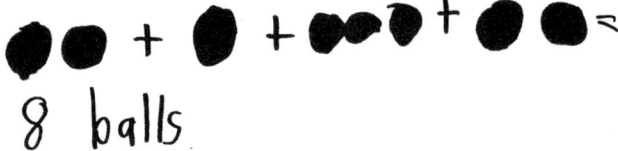

Solution

The Wordly girl has eight bouncy balls.

The Birthday Party

Word Problem

One of the Wordly boys had a birthday party. Five friends carpooled together in a van. Two friends walked over. Three friends rode their bikes. Alex's dad drove over late and dropped him off.

How many children came by car?

Talk About It

- Are we trying to find out how many children came to the party? What is the question?
- Can we count the three friends that rode their bikes?

Use Symbols   *Materials: paper and pencil*

Make a tally for everyone who came by car. Count the number of tallies.

car //////

Solution

Six children came to the birthday party by car.

©Primary Concepts   Word Problem of the Day

The Biggest Cat

Word Problem

The Wordlys have three cats. The *spotted* cat is *smaller* than the cat that is all gray. The gray cat is smaller than the *striped* cat.

Which cat is the *biggest*?

Talk About It

- What does it mean when a cat has stripes? What does *spotted* mean?
- If the black cat is smaller than the gray cat, which one is *bigger*?

Picture It   *Materials: paper and pencil*

Draw the spotted cat, the gray cat, and the striped cat so you can compare their sizes.

Solution

The striped cat is biggest.

The Ice Cream Truck

Word Problem

The ice cream truck came down the street near the Wordly house. Three neighbor children—Niki, Karina, and Megan—heard the truck and ran to get ice cream. Karina was *first* in line. Megan was *last*.

Where was Niki?

Talk About It

- Why were the girls standing in line?
- Who is *closest* to the ice cream truck? (Karina)
- Who is *farthest* away? (Megan)

Act It Out

Work with two partners. One of you can be Megan. One can be Karina. One can be Niki. A desk can be the ice cream truck.

Solution

Karina is first, nearest the truck. Niki is *next*, and Megan is last. So Niki is in the *middle*, *between* the other girls. She is *second* in line.

Three Balls

Word Problem

One of the Wordly boys had two friends over. He brought out a red ball, a blue ball, and a green ball. Matt said, "I'll take *either* the red ball *or* the green ball." Kip said, "I want a red ball."

Which ball does the Wordly boy get?

Talk About It

- How many boys are there altogether? (three)
- Are there *enough* balls for each boy to get one? (yes)
- What does it mean to want a red or a green ball? Does it mean that you get *both* balls?

Use Symbols   *Materials: paper and crayons or markers*

Draw circles to represent the three balls. Cross off the balls that the Wordly boy can't have. Which one is left?

Solution

The Wordly boy gets the blue ball.

Who Set the Table?

Word Problem

When Mrs. Wordly sets the table, she folds the napkins to form a *rectangle*. Mr. Wordly folds the napkins differently. When the children look at the table, they always know which parent set the table by the *shape* of the napkins. Today the napkins have three *sides*.

What shape are the napkins? Who set the table?

Talk About It

- What shape are the napkins to start? (squares)
- What shape does Mrs. Wordly form? (rectangle)

Do It   *Materials: square napkins or square pieces of paper*

Fold the napkin in two ways. What shapes can you make with one fold? (a rectangle and a triangle) How many sides does a rectangle have? How many sides does a triangle have?

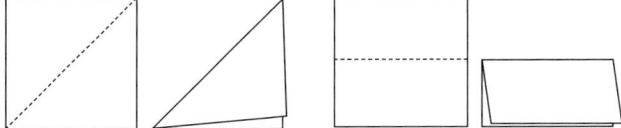

Solution

If the napkin has three sides, it is shaped like a *triangle*. Mr. Wordly set the table.

14

An Amazing Sight

Word Problem

There are three steps leading up to the Wordlys' front door. One day, the Wordlys came home to an amazing sight. Three of the family pets were sitting on the front steps. Each animal was on a different step. The dog was on the *top* step. The rabbit was on the *middle* step.

Where was the cat?

Talk About It

- Could the cat be on the same step as the dog or the rabbit? Explain.
- Do we know how many front steps there are at the Wordly house? (yes, three)

Picture It   Materials: paper and crayons or markers

Draw three lines for the steps. Draw to show where the dog was. Draw where the rabbit was. Draw where the cat was.

Solution

The cat was on the *bottom* step.

More Pennies in the Jar

Word Problem

The Wordly *penny* jar is getting full. One day, Mrs. Wordly had three pennies to put in. Mr. Wordly said, "I've got four *more* pennies *than* you do."

How many pennies in all will Mr. and Mrs. Wordly put in the penny jar?

Talk About It

- Who has more pennies? (Mr. Wordly)
- Did Mr. Wordly say how many pennies he has? (no)
- What clues can help us figure out how many pennies he has? (four more pennies than Mrs. Wordly)
- What is the question?

Show It   *Materials: counters or pennies*

Show the number of pennies Mrs. Wordly has. Then show the number of pennies Mr. Wordly has (three and four more). Then count how many pennies there are altogether.

Solution

There are ten pennies altogether (three from Mrs. Wordly and seven from Mr. Wordly).

16

Performance Assessment

Word Problem

One of the Wordly children is nine years old today, and Mrs. Wordly is baking a cake. She is worried that she will have to run to the store and buy more candles. She counts out two blue candles. There are three green candles. There are two red candles. And there is one pink candle.

Are there enough candles?

Talk About It

- Why does Mrs. Wordly need candles?
- How many candles does she need? (nine)
- If she had ten candles, would that be enough? (yes)

Solve It   *Materials: paper and crayons or markers*

Use pictures and words to show your answer.

[Student work: II + III + III + I = 8]
No, thar are not enuf candles.

Solution

There are eight candles and Mrs. Wordly needs nine. There are not enough candles.

Home Sweet Home

Word Problem

Mrs. Wordly has some beautiful ceramic tiles with a letter painted on each one. She wants to put a welcome sign beside their front door. The sign will read *HOME SWEET HOME*. There are three of each letter of the alphabet in her set of tiles.

Does Mrs. Wordly have *enough* tiles to spell *HOME SWEET HOME*?

Talk About It

- What are ceramic tiles? Have you ever seen tiles like those Mrs. Wordly has?
- If Mrs. Wordly needs two of a letter, would she have enough? three? four?

Make a List   *Materials: paper and pencil*

Make a list of the letters Mrs. Wordly will need. Count the number of each letter she will use.

h	o	m	e	s	w	t
2	2	2	4	1	1	1

Solution

One set of three letters will *not* be *enough*. She needs four *E*'s for the sign.

©Primary Concepts   Word Problem of the Day

Shapes in a Rug

Word Problem

The rug in the Wordly family room has an interesting design. It is the *shape* of a *square*. There is fringe around the *outside* of the rug. *Inside* the square is a *circle*. Inside the circle is another square. In the *center* is a star.

What does the Wordly rug look like?

Talk About It

- What is the shape of the rug? (square)
- What is fringe?

Picture It   *Materials: paper and pencil*

Draw a picture of the rug. Draw the outside shape (a square). Draw fringe around the *edge*. Then draw the design.

Solution

The rug looks like this:

Forming Teams

Word Problem

The oldest Wordly boy and his five best friends want to play a soccer game. First, they need to form two *even* teams.

Can the boys form two even teams?

Talk About It

- What does it mean when teams have an even number of players?
- How many boys want to play? (six)
- Do we need to know which team the Wordly boy will be on to answer the question? (no)

Act It Out

Get into a group of six children. Divide up into even teams.

Solution

Yes, they can form two even teams: three on one team and three on the other.

Uncle Nate's Farm

Word Problem

The Wordly family went to visit Uncle Nate on vacation. Uncle Nate has lots of animals. There were the horses: Coffee, Sunrise, and Needles. There was Shola, the sheep. There was the mama pig and her seven piglets.

How many farm animals does Uncle Nate have?

Talk About It

- What are some ways we could solve this problem?
- Should Uncle Nate be counted in the total? Explain.
- How many pigs were there in all? (eight)

Use Symbols   *Materials: paper and pencil*

Make a tally to represent each farm animal. Then count the tallies.

Solution

There were 12 farm animals in all.

The Last Appointment

Word Problem

Mrs. Wordly told three of the Wordly children that she had appointments for them at the dentist. The appointments were at two, three, and four *o'clock*. One of the children said he wanted to take the appointment at three o'clock. Another child said she would take an *earlier* appointment. The youngest child had to take what was left.

What time will the youngest child go to the dentist?

Talk About It

- What is an appointment? Why are the appointments at different times?
- How many children are going to the dentist? (three)

Make a List   *Materials: paper and pencil*

Write down the three times that are available. Cross off times that are taken. What time is left?

Solution

The youngest child will go at four o'clock, the *latest* appointment.

Sharing Cookies

Word Problem

Mrs. Wordly made a batch of a *dozen* cookies. "Who wants some cookies?" she called out. Three of the Wordly children and Mr. Wordly came running to the kitchen. Mrs. Wordly didn't want to eat any cookies. "You need to *share equally*," she said.

How many cookies does each person get if they share them equally?

Talk About It

- How many people are sharing the cookies? (four)
- How many is a dozen?
- What does it mean to share the cookies equally?

Show It   *Materials: counters*

Work in a group of four. Use counters to represent the cookies. Find a way to share the counters equally. Count how many each of you has.

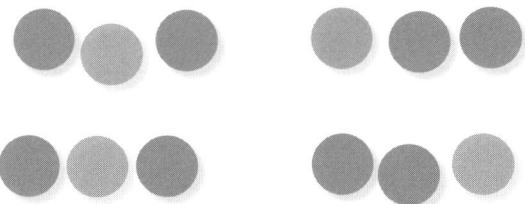

Solution

Each person gets three cookies.

Collecting Rocks

Word Problem

The youngest Wordly boy picks up interesting rocks on his way home from school. He keeps the rocks in an old shoe box. He has six *spotted* rocks and two *striped* rocks.

How many *more* spotted rocks *than* striped rocks does the Wordly boy have?

Talk About It

- Are we trying to find out how many rocks the Wordly boy has in all? What is the question?
- If there were the *same* number of spotted rocks as striped rocks, how many spotted rocks would there be? (two)

Picture It   *Materials: paper and pencil*

Draw the rocks in *rows*. Line up the rocks to compare the numbers. Count how many more spotted rocks there are.

Solution

The Wordly boy has four more spotted rocks than striped rocks.

Performance Assessment

Word Problem

The youngest Wordly boy found a bug in the backyard. He counted three legs on one side. "This must be a spider," he said.

Is he right?

Talk About It

- How many legs does a spider have? (eight)
- What information do we know about the bug's legs? (that there are three legs on one side)
- What do we need to know? (how many legs are on both sides)
- Would the number of legs on each side be the same?

Solve It   *Materials: paper and pencil*

Use pictures and words to show your answer.

Solution

No, the Wordly boy is wrong. The bug has six legs. It is not a spider.

Dad's Trip

Word Problem

Mr. Wordly likes to play guessing games with the children. One Sunday, Mr. Wordly was about to leave on a trip when one of the girls asked, "Dad, when are you coming home?" He said, "I won't be gone *more than* three nights, and I'm not coming home on *Monday* or *Wednesday*." His daughter groaned, "I'll check the *calendar*."

What day is Mr. Wordly coming home?

Talk About It

- Let's name the *days of the week* in order. Sunday, Monday,…
- On which day of the week does Mr. Wordly leave? (Sunday)
- What day comes *next*? (Monday)
- Could he come back that day? (no)

Do It   *Materials: class calendar and sticky notes*

Use a calendar. Let's put sticky notes on the days Mr. Wordly will *not* be traveling. Which day is left?

Solution

Mr. Wordly will be coming home on *Tuesday*.

Kickball

Word Problem

At school, the teacher told the children that she wanted to form two *even* teams for a game of kickball. There were 15 children in class that day.

Is it possible to make two even teams? If so, how many are on each team?

Talk About It

- What does it mean to have even teams?
- What are some different ways to figure out how many children would be on each team?
- What are even numbers?

Picture It   *Materials: paper and pencil*

Draw a quick stick figure sketch of a player for one team and then a player for the other team. Line up the players you draw so that you can see that they are even. Keep going until you get to 15 players in all.

Team A

Team B

Solution

It is not possible to make even teams. One team would have eight players, and the other team would have seven players.

The Photograph

Word Problem

The Wordlys have a photograph that shows the two teenagers and their parents. In the photograph, one of the teenagers is *taller* than his father. The other teenager is *shorter* than his dad but taller than his mother.

Who in the photograph is the *shortest*?

Talk About It

- How many people are in the photograph? (four)
- Who is shorter than you are? Who is taller?
- If you are the *tallest*, is anyone taller than you are?

Use Symbols   *Materials: paper and pencil*

Draw lines to represent the heights of the different people in the photograph. Show one teenager taller than his dad. Show the other teenager shorter than his dad but taller than his mom. Mark the lines with an *M* and a *D* to show who is mom and who is dad.

Solution

Mom is the shortest one in the photograph.

Pocket Change

Word Problem

One of the Wordly children is just like his father. He likes to play guessing games. One day, his sister asked him if he had any money in his pocket. He said, "I have two *silver coins* in my pocket. One is worth five *cents*. The other one is *smaller* in size."

What coins did he have?

Talk About It

- How many coins does the Wordly boy have? (two)
- Could he have a *penny* in his pocket? (no, because a penny is not silver)
- What do we know about the coins he has?

Show It   Materials: play money—coins

Find a coin that is worth five cents. Then find a coin that is smaller in size.

Solution

The Wordly boy had a *nickel* and a *dime* in his pocket.

Dance Steps

Word Problem

The family watched as one of the Wordly children showed them how to do the steps of a line dance. First she walked *forward* one step. Then she turned to the *right* and walked one step. Then she turned to the *left* and walked one step. Then she turned to the left again and walked one step. Then she turned to the right and walked one step. Then she walked *backward* three steps.

Where did she end up?

Talk About It

- Which way is right? Which way is left?
- Which way is forward? Which way is backward?

Act It Out

Follow the steps. Where do you end up?

Solution

The Wordly girl ended up exactly where she started.

The Petting Zoo

Word Problem

One day the Wordlys went to a petting zoo. They got to pet a turtle, a mountain goat, a rooster, a chipmunk, a barn owl, a miniature pony, and a gigantic beetle from South America. "*Most* of the animals have four legs," said one of the Wordly children on the way home.

Was he right? Did most of the animals at the petting zoo have four legs?

Talk About It

- Who has been to a petting zoo before?
- Does a beetle have four legs? an owl? a turtle?

Make a List   *Materials: paper and pencil*

Make a list with two *columns*. In one column, list the animals that have four legs. In the other column, list the animals that do not have four legs. Which list is *longer*?

yes	no
turtle	chicken
goat	owl
chipmunk	beetle
pony	

Solution

Yes, most of the animals at the petting zoo have four legs.

Cake for Mom

Word Problem

The Wordly children are baking a cake for Mrs. Wordly's birthday. They have a box of candy letters with two of each letter of the alphabet. They want to use the letters to spell out the words *HAPPY BIRTHDAY, MOM* on the cake.

Will they have *enough* letters to spell *HAPPY BIRTHDAY, MOM*?

Talk About It

- How many letters do they have to start? (two of each)
- There are 52 letters in the box. Why wouldn't they have enough? (if more than two of a letter is needed)
- How could we figure out if they have enough letters?

Make a List   *Materials: paper and pencil*

Make a list of the letters the Wordly children will need. Count the number of each letter they will use.

H	A	P	Y	B	I	R	T	D	M	O
2	2	2	2	1	1	1	1	1	2	1

Solution

There are enough letters. Two letters are needed for *H, A, P, Y,* and *M*. The rest need only one letter. They do not need more than two of any of the letters.

Performance Assessment

Word Problem

One of the Wordly boys is trying to figure out which of his three friends is tallest. His friend Luis is shorter than his friend Alex. His friend Jason is shorter than Luis.

Who is the tallest boy: Jason, Alex, or Luis?

Talk About It

- Think of a friend. Who's taller, you or your friend?
- Think of three friends. Who is tallest?

Solve It   *Materials: paper and crayons or markers*

Use pictures and words to show your answer.

Solution

Alex is the tallest boy.

Fruit for Lunch

Word Problem

Mrs. Wordly is making lunches for six children. She wants to put fruit in each lunch. She has a pear, three apples, two bananas, and a peach.

Does she have *enough* fruit?

Talk About It

- How much would be enough? (six)
- If she had five pieces of fruit, would that be enough? six? seven?
- To answer the question, is it important to know what fruit goes in what bag? (no)

Picture It   *Materials: paper and pencil*

Draw the lunch bags in a row. Then draw a picture of each fruit. Now draw lines from the fruit to a bag. Does each bag get fruit?

Solution

There are *more than enough* pieces of fruit for the lunches (seven fruits for six lunch bags).

The Soccer Team

Word Problem

One of the Wordly children is on a soccer team. They need eight children to play. So far, four boys have shown up. *Fewer* girls have shown up.

Does the team have *enough* players?

Talk About It

- Do we know how many boys there are? (yes, four boys)
- What do we know about how many girls there are? (*less than* four; *either* three, two, *or* one)
- How many children are needed for this team? (eight)

Act It Out

Let's have four boys stand in front of the room. Now let's have fewer girls stand in front of the room. If we have three girls, are there enough? What about two girls? one girl?

Solution

The team does *not* have *enough* players.

A Crate for Lulu

Word Problem

The Wordlys are shopping for a crate for their Chihuahua, Lulu. The dog needs to be able to stand up in the crate. Lulu is 7 *inches tall*. The crates they are looking at are 6 inches, 10 inches, and 12 inches tall. They want to get the *shortest* crate possible.

Which crate should they buy?

Talk About It

- About how big is an inch?
- Are we looking for the number of inches that is closest to 7? Explain.
- Are we looking for the *tallest* crate? Explain.

Show It   *Materials: ruler*

Find on a *ruler* where 7 inches is. Then find the crate sizes on the ruler. Which one is best?

Solution

The 10-inch crate is the best one to buy.

A Picky Eater

Word Problem

Lulu, the Wordlys' dog, is a picky eater. She likes only dog food in cans, and she will eat only beef and chicken flavors. The Wordlys are going on vacation for a *week*. In the cupboard, they have two cans of beef, three cans of chicken, and five cans of turkey. Lulu eats one can of dog food each day.

Does Mrs. Wordly need to buy *more* dog food for their pet sitter?

Talk About It

- How long are the Wordlys gone on vacation? (a week)
- How many days are in a week?
- Will Lulu eat turkey? (no)

Use Symbols   *Materials: paper and pencil*

Make a tally for each can of dog food that Lulu will eat. Count the tallies.

Solution

Mrs. Wordly does need to buy more dog food. (There are only five cans that Lulu will eat. She needs to buy at least two more cans of beef or chicken flavor.)

Squares in a Quilt

Word Problem

Mrs. Wordly is making a quilt. The directions say to cut a *square* piece of cloth to make three *triangles*. Mrs. Wordly cannot figure out how to do this. One of her daughters said, "I get it. You'll have one *big* triangle and two *small* ones."

How should Mrs. Wordly cut the square?

Talk About It

- How are quilts made?
- What is a square? What is a triangle?
- Can you cut a square to make two triangles? Explain.

Make a Model   *Materials: square paper, pencils, and scissors*

Fold, cut, or draw on square paper. Find a way to make the triangles.

Solution

Cut the paper in *half* on a *diagonal*, and then cut one of the halves in half.

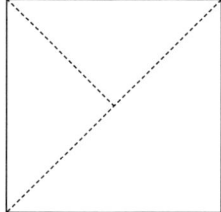

Doctor's Appointment

Word Problem

Mrs. Wordly needs to make a doctor's appointment after school for the oldest Wordly girl. After school, the oldest Wordly girl has piano lessons on *Tuesdays*, softball practice on *Wednesdays*, and chorus on *Mondays*.

On which *days of the week* is the Wordly girl free?

Talk About It

- Which days of the week are school days?
- Is Mrs. Wordly thinking about making an appointment on a *Saturday* or *Sunday*?
- Will Mrs. Wordly make an appointment when the Wordly girl is busy after school?

Make a List   Materials: paper and pencil

Make a list of the days of the school week. Write down when the Wordly girl is busy.

Solution

Mrs. Wordly can make the doctor's appointment on a *Thursday* or a *Friday* after school.

Pieces on a Game Board

Word Problem

The youngest Wordly girl and her friend were playing a board game. On her *first* move, the Wordly girl moved *forward* four spaces. On her *second* turn, she moved forward six spaces. On her *third* turn, she went *backward* five spaces.

After her third turn, how far was the Wordly girl from Start?

Talk About It

- Before her first move, where is the Wordly girl's playing piece? (at Start)
- If the Wordly girl moves her playing piece forward, does she move *closer* to or *farther* from Start?
- If the Wordly girl moves her playing piece backward, does she move closer to or farther from Start?

Picture It   *Materials: paper and pencil*

Draw a path on a game board using squares. Label the first square Start. Mark an X showing where the Wordly girl lands after her third move.

Solution

The Wordly girl is five spaces from Start.

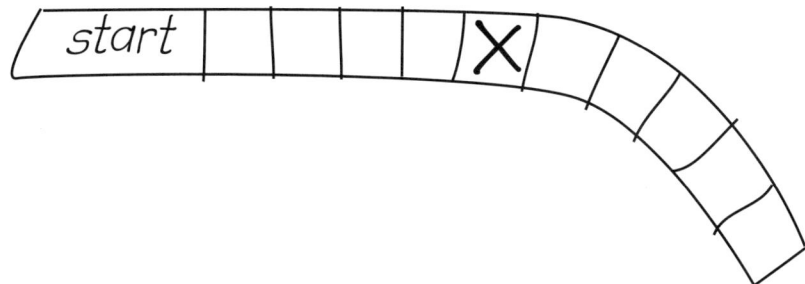

Performance Assessment

Word Problem

One of the Wordly girls is having a birthday soon. She would like to give a cupcake to each child in her class, plus one for her teacher, too. There are 18 children in her class. Cupcakes come in packs, with a dozen cupcakes in each pack.

How many cupcakes should the Wordlys buy?

Talk About It

- How many cupcakes does the girl need? (19)
- Can she buy exactly that many? (no, cupcakes come only in packs of one dozen)
- How many is a dozen?

Solve It   *Materials: paper and pencil*

Use pictures and words to show your answer.

Solution

The Wordlys will need to buy two dozen (24) cupcakes even though they need only 19 cupcakes.

Stuffed Animals

Word Problem

The youngest Wordly girl has 11 stuffed animals. She has one rabbit, one duck, three dogs, and the rest cats.

How many cats does she have?

Talk About It

- Do you own any stuffed animals? What kind of stuffed animals do you have?
- Are we trying to find out how many different types of animals the Wordly girl has? What question are we trying to answer?
- How can we find the answer?

Picture It   *Materials: paper and pencil*

Write the numbers 1 to 11 across your paper. Under each number, draw one of the stuffed animals. Count the number of cats you drew.

Solution

The Wordly girl has six stuffed cats.

The Overdue Book

Word Problem

The youngest Wordly boy had checked out a book about pirates from the school library. The book was due on *Monday*. He forgot to bring it to school. He did not return the book until *Friday*!

How many days was the book overdue?

Talk About It

- What does *overdue* mean?
- Have you ever forgotten to return a library book?

Do It   *Materials: class calendar and sticky notes*

Use a calendar. Let's put a sticky note on each day of the week that the library book was overdue. On which day of the week does the first sticky note go? the last? Now let's count the number of sticky notes.

Solution

The book was overdue four days.

Pajama Drawer

Word Problem

The youngest Wordly boy's dresser holds his pajamas, pants, and shirts. The dresser has three drawers. Each type of clothing is in a separate drawer. The *middle* drawer holds his shirts. His pants are in the *bottom* drawer.

In which drawer are his pajamas?

Talk About It

- Are his pants and pajamas in the same drawer? (no)
- How many drawers are there? (three)
- How many different types of clothing are there? (three)

Picture It   *Materials: paper and pencil*

Draw three drawers. Draw to show where the shirts are. Draw where the pants are. Draw where the pajamas are.

Solution

The pajamas are in the *top* drawer.

Lulu and the Cat Toys

Word Problem

The Wordlys' dog Lulu likes to hide the cats' toys *inside* her doghouse. She already has five cat toys inside her doghouse. There are seven cat toys in all.

How many cat toys are *outside* the doghouse?

Talk About It

- What does Lulu do with the cats' toys?
- If Lulu hides seven cat toys inside her doghouse, how many cat toys will be outside the doghouse? (*none* or *zero*)

Show It   *Materials: paper, pencil, and counters*

Draw a large doghouse on the piece of paper. Count out seven counters to represent the cat toys. Put five counters in the doghouse. Count the number left outside the doghouse.

Solution

There are two cat toys outside the doghouse.

Birthday Balloons

Word Problem

Mrs. Wordly is buying balloons for the middle Wordly girl's birthday. She needs 11 balloons. She asks the clerk, "May I have two blue balloons, three greens, a purple, two yellows,...." Then Mrs. Wordly gets confused. "How many balloons is that?"

Has Mrs. Wordly asked for *enough* balloons?

Talk About It

- What is Mrs. Wordly buying? Why?
- If she has asked for ten balloons, is that enough? Explain.
- Is the color of the balloons important for solving the problem?

Picture It   *Materials: paper and crayons or markers*

Draw the balloons Mrs. Wordly has asked for. Count how many balloons there are.

Solution

No, Mrs. Wordly has asked for only eight balloons. She needs three more. There are *not enough* balloons yet.

Worm Tally

Word Problem

One morning after a rain, the youngest Wordly children were out counting worms. The Wordly girl said, "I think we'll find *more than* 15 worms today!" They found six worms in the driveway. There were six worms on the walkway. The Wordly boy found two worms on the sidewalk.

Was the youngest Wordly girl right? Did they find more than 15 worms?

Talk About It

- What were the youngest Wordly children doing? Have you ever seen worms after a rain?
- If they found *exactly* 15 worms, would she be right?
- How can we find the answer?

Use Symbols   *Materials: paper and pencil*

Make a tally for each worm the youngest Wordly children found. Count the tallies.

Solution

No, the youngest Wordly girl is not right. The Wordlys found *less than* 15 worms. They found only 14 worms.

The Orange Cat

Word Problem

The youngest Wordly girl wants to earn some extra money to buy a new stuffed animal—an orange cat. The cat *costs* $14. She earned $5 for raking the leaves in the yard and $2 for washing the car. She already had four $1 bills in a box in her room.

Does she have *enough* money to buy the cat?

Talk About It

- What does the Wordly girl want to buy?
- Do you ever do extra tasks at home to earn money?
- How much money does she have in her box? ($4)
- How can we figure out the answer?

Show It   *Materials: play money—dollar bills*

Count out the amount of money the Wordly girl has. Is it enough?

Solution

The Wordly girl does *not* have *enough* money to buy the cat. She has only $11.

Performance Assessment

Word Problem

While cleaning his room, the youngest Wordly boy found eight sports figures. He found two basketball players, three baseball players, and the rest football players.

How many football players did the Wordly boy find?

Talk About It

- What did the Wordly boy find while cleaning his room? Do you own any sports figures?
- What different types of sports figures did the Wordly boy find?
- Are we trying to find how many sports figures he found? What question are we trying to answer?

Solve It   *Materials: paper and crayons or markers*

Use pictures and words to show your answer.

Solution

The Wordly boy found three football players.

Hungry for Pizza

Word Problem

The Wordlys ordered two extra large pizzas for dinner. Each pizza was cut into eight pieces. The pizzas were sitting on the counter when the oldest Wordly boy got home from basketball practice. "I'm so hungry I could eat *half* a pizza!" said the Wordly boy.

How many pieces of pizza did the Wordly boy think he could eat?

Talk About It

- Do we need to know how many pieces of pizza there were in all?
- What information do we need to solve the problem?
- How much is "half" of something?

Picture It   *Materials: paper and pencil*

Draw a circle to represent one of the pizzas. Mark lines to cut the pizza into eight equal pieces. Shade half the pizza. Count the number of pieces you shaded.

Solution

The Wordly boy thought he could eat four pieces of pizza.

The Field Trip

Word Problem

The youngest Wordly boy's class was going on a field trip to the space museum. His teacher *paired* up the students so each would have a buddy. There are 18 students in the Wordly boy's class, but 2 students were sick and did not come.

How many pairs of students were there?

Talk About It

- Where was the Wordly boy's class going?
- What does *paired up* mean?
- What question are we trying to answer?
- How can we find out how many students went on the field trip?

Show It   Materials: counters

Use counters to represent the students. Pair up the counters to find the number of pairs.

Solution

There were eight pairs of students on the field trip.

Bagels for the Team

Word Problem

Mrs. Wordly brought a *dozen* bagels and cream cheese for the youngest Wordly girl's soccer game. The *twins*, Maria, and the Wordly girl all ate a bagel. The rest of the team ate cupcakes that another family brought.

How many bagels were left over?

Talk About It

- How many bagels are there in a dozen?
- What is a twin?
- How many girls ate bagels? (four)

Use Symbols   *Materials: paper and pencil*

Make a circle to represent each bagel. Mark an X for each bagel that a player ate.

Solution

There were eight bagels left over.

Fish for the Aquarium

Word Problem

The middle Wordly boy bought some new fish for his aquarium. He got four *spotted* fish. He got one *plain* fish. He got two *fewer striped* fish than spotted fish.

How many new fish did the Wordly boy buy altogether?

Talk About It

- What did the Wordly boy buy?
- Did the Wordly boy buy more spotted fish or striped fish?
- How can we figure out how many striped fish the Wordly boy bought?

Picture It   *Materials: paper and crayons or markers*

Draw the spotted fish, the plain fish, and the striped fish. Count the number of fish.

Solution

The Wordly boy bought seven fish in all.

The Necklace

Word Problem

The youngest Wordly girl was making a beaded necklace, using three colors of beads. She strung the beads in this *pattern:* green, yellow, blue, green, yellow, blue.

What color was the *eighth* bead?

Talk About It

- What is the Wordly girl making?
- What is a pattern?
- What color bead comes *after* blue in the Wordly girl's pattern?

Find a Pattern   *Materials: paper and crayons or markers*

Draw the first eight beads in the pattern.

Solution

The eighth bead is yellow.

Cold and Colder

Word Problem

Mr. Wordly looked through the window at the outdoor *thermometer* and said, "I hope it warms up. If it gets one *degree* colder, I will have to cover up the plants." He always covers up the outdoor plants when the *temperature* hits 32 degrees.

What is the temperature outdoors?

Talk About It

- Do you know what happens when the temperature is below 32 degrees?
- What is a thermometer?
- Why is Mr. Wordly checking the thermometer?
- Is it *colder* or *hotter* than 32 degrees?

Do It   Materials: thermometer

Look at a thermometer. Find the temperature that is one degree warmer than freezing.

Solution

It is 33 degrees outdoors.

Lines at the Movie

Word Problem

On Saturday, the Wordlys decided to see a movie. When they went to the movie theater, there were three lines to get tickets. Four people stood in the line on the *left*. The *middle* line had two *more* people than the line on the left. The line on the *right* had three *fewer* people than the line in the middle. Mr. Wordly wanted to stand in the *shortest* line.

Which line was shortest?

Talk About It

- Where were the Wordlys going? Why do you think Mr. Wordly wanted to stand in the shortest line?
- Have you ever stood in a really long line? When?
- If one line is *longer* than a second line, does the first line have more or fewer people than the second line? (more)

Act It Out

Let's have four students stand in a line in front of the room. Now let's make the middle line that has two more students in it than the line on the left. Then let's make a line on the right that has three fewer students than the line in the middle.

Solution

The line on the right is shortest. (There are three people standing in line.)

©Primary Concepts

Performance Assessment

Word Problem

One Saturday, the Wordlys went to their neighborhood block party. They brought three small pies to share: pumpkin, chocolate, and apple. Each pie was cut into six equal pieces. Mr. Wordly ate a hamburger and a huge salad. When he went to get a piece of pie, there was only half an apple pie left. The rest of the pies were all eaten!

How many pieces of pie were left?

Talk About It

- What is a neighborhood block party? Has anyone ever been to one?
- What did the Wordlys bring to share?
- Could Mr. Wordly have a piece of chocolate pie?
- What does *half* mean?

Solve It   *Materials: paper and crayons or markers*

Use pictures and words to show your answer.

Solution

There were three pieces of pie left.

Lucky Day

Word Problem

It was the oldest Wordly boy's lucky day! While he was walking home from school, he found three *coins* on the ground. All the coins were different. The *largest* coin was worth five *cents*.

How much money did the Wordly boy find?

Talk About It

- What did the Wordly boy find?
- Could the largest coin be a *quarter*? (no, because the largest coin is worth five cents)
- Are any of the coins the *same*? (no)
- Does the question ask us to name the other coins? (no, to find the amount of money in all)

Show It   *Materials: play money—coins*

Find a coin that is worth five cents. Find two other different coins that are *smaller* than it. Count to find the amount in all.

Solution

The Wordly boy found 16 cents in all (a *nickel*, a *dime*, and a *penny*).

Eggs for Breakfast

Word Problem

One Sunday morning, Mr. Wordly wanted to make omelets for breakfast. "There are eight eggs in the refrigerator. I will need *half* of them to make the omelets." The middle Wordly girl said, "But I need two eggs to make cookies for the band performance tonight." Mrs. Wordly added, "And I need two eggs for dinner."

Are there *enough* eggs for everyone?

Talk About It

- Who has had an omelet before? What is it?
- What does *half* mean?
- Does the question ask how many eggs the Wordlys will use in all? What does the question ask?

Picture It   *Materials: paper and pencil*

Draw the number of eggs in the refrigerator. Mark an X on each egg that the Wordlys need.

Solution

Yes, there are just enough eggs.

Wheel Count

Word Problem

Mr. Wordly was cleaning the garage one Saturday morning. "Wow!" he thought. "There are a lot of things with wheels in here." There were three bicycles, two tricycles, one wagon, and one unicycle.

How many wheels were there in all?

Talk About It

- Who can describe what a unicycle is? How many wheels does a unicycle have?
- How many wheels does a tricycle have?
- How many wheels does a wagon have?

Use Symbols   *Materials: paper and pencil*

Make a circle to represent each wheel. Count the number of wheels.

Solution

There are 17 wheels altogether.

Buttons on a Dress

Word Problem

Grandma Wordly is sewing a dress for the oldest Wordly girl. The front of the dress has buttons down the *front*, in three different *shapes*. The *top* button is *square*. Next is a *circle*. Next is a *triangle*. She wants to continue this *pattern* to the *bottom* of the dress.

If the dress has seven buttons, what shape button will be at the bottom?

Talk About It

- Are all the buttons the same shape? (no)
- Why do you think Grandma Wordly might want to follow a pattern with the buttons?

Find a Pattern   *Materials: paper and pencil*

Draw a picture of the dress. Show the shapes of the seven buttons.

Solution

The bottom button will be a square.

Fruit Juice for Friends

Word Problem

The youngest Wordly girl and her two friends are thirsty. There are three juice boxes in the refrigerator: apple, berry, and fruit punch. Karina said, "I want berry." Sophia said, "I do not want *either* fruit punch *or* berry."

Which juice box is left for the Wordly girl?

Talk About It

- Are there enough juice boxes for each girl to have one? (yes)
- What does it mean not to want either fruit punch or berry?
- Which juice box will Sophia drink? (apple)

Use Symbols   *Materials: paper and pencil*

Make a rectangle to represent each juice box. Cross off the juice boxes that the Wordly girl cannot have. Which one is left?

Solution

The Wordly girl gets fruit punch.

Wedding Shoes

Word Problem

One of the Wordlys' cousins is getting married in the afternoon, and the Wordlys are getting dressed to go. The youngest Wordly boy has two pairs of dressy shoes. One pair of shoes is brown, and one pair is black. He has three pairs of dressy socks. The socks are green, blue, and gray. "Hurry up and get your shoes on," Mrs. Wordly sang out. "It's almost time to go."

What choices does the Wordly boy have for shoes and socks?

Talk About It

- What are the choices for shoes? (black or brown)
- What are the choices for socks? (green or blue or gray)
- What is one *combination* of shoes and socks he could wear?

Make a List   Materials: paper and crayons or markers

Make a list of pictures showing each of the choices.

Solution

There are six different combinations of shoes and socks:

>black shoes and green socks
>black shoes and blue socks
>black shoes and gray socks
>
>brown shoes and green socks
>brown shoes and blue socks
>brown shoes and gray socks

Word Problem of the Day   ©Primary Concepts

A Package of Pencils

Word Problem

Two of the Wordly children need new pencils for school. Mr. Wordly bought a package of 24 pencils. When Mrs. Wordly saw the package, she said, "I need some new pencils, too." Mr. Wordly said, "You must *share* these pencils *equally*."

How many pencils will each Wordly get if they share the pencils equally?

Talk About It

- What did Mr. Wordly buy?
- How many Wordlys need new pencils? (three)
- What does it mean to share equally?

Show It   *Materials: craft sticks*

Work in a group of three. Use craft sticks to represent the pencils. Find a way to share the pencils equally. Count how many each of you has.

Solution

Each Wordly gets eight pencils.

©Primary Concepts

Performance Assessment

Word Problem

Mr. Wordly found four coins while cleaning the van. All the coins were silver. Two coins were the same and were the smallest coins. None of the coins was worth more than 25 cents.

What coins did Mr. Wordly find?

Talk About It

- What did Mr. Wordly find while cleaning the van?
- Could one of the coins be a penny?
- Could one of the coins be a half dollar coin?
- Are we trying to find out how much money Mr. Wordly found? What question are we trying to answer?

Solve It   *Materials: paper and crayons or markers*

Use pictures and words to show your answer.

Solution

Mr. Wordly found a nickel, two dimes, and a quarter.

The Garden

Word Problem

The warm weather had finally arrived, so Mr. Wordly decided to plant a vegetable garden. He bought 13 plants. He wanted to plant them in 3 *rows* with an *equal* number of plants in each row.

Can he plant the *same* number in each row?

Talk About It

- What is Mr. Wordly going to plant?
- How does he want to plant his vegetable garden? (in 3 rows with an equal number in each row)
- What does *an equal number in each row* mean?

Show It   *Materials: counters*

Use counters to represent the plants. Put the counters into three even rows if possible. Are there any counters left over?

Solution

Mr. Wordly cannot plant the same number in each row. He can put four plants in each row, but there is one plant left over.

Visiting Uncle Nate

Word Problem

Last summer the oldest Wordly boy went by himself to visit Uncle Nate. The Wordly boy left on *Tuesday* and returned home on *Sunday*.

How many nights was the Wordly boy gone?

Talk About It

- Where did the Wordly boy go?
- What information do we know? (left on Tuesday, came home on Sunday)
- What are the *days of the week,* starting with Sunday?
- Was the Wordly boy gone on Tuesday night? How about Sunday night?

Do It   Materials: class calendar and sticky notes

Use a calendar. Let's put sticky notes on the day the Wordly boy left and the day he came home. Now let's count the number of nights he was gone.

Solution

The Wordly boy was gone for five nights.

Jumping Contest

Word Problem

The youngest Wordly boy and his two friends had a jumping contest to see who could jump the *farthest*. Tim jumped *farther* than the Wordly boy. Juan jumped the *shortest* distance.

Who jumped the farthest?

Talk About It

- What were the Wordly boy and his friends doing?
- How many boys jumped in the contest? (three)
- Did the Wordly boy jump the farthest? Explain.

Act It Out

Let's pick three students to represent the three boys. Here's the starting line. Now show where the Wordly boy might have jumped. Next, show where the Juan could have jumped. Finally, where could Tim have jumped?

Solution

Tim jumped the farthest.

©Primary Concepts · Word Problem of the Day

The Striped Rug

Word Problem

The rug in the Wordly children's bathroom is *striped*. It has ten stripes. The *first* stripe is blue. The *second* and *third* stripes are yellow. This *pattern* continues.

What color is the *last* stripe?

Talk About It

- What design did the bathroom rug have?
- What does *this patterned continued* mean? What is the pattern?
- What color is the *fourth* stripe? (blue)

Find a Pattern   Materials: paper and crayons or markers

Draw the Wordlys' bathroom rug. Draw the first stripe blue, the second stripe yellow, and the third stripe yellow. Continue this pattern until you've drawn ten stripes in all.

Solution

The last stripe is blue.

```
B  Y  Y  B  Y  Y  B  Y  Y  B
1  2  3  4  5  6  7  8  9  10
```

Word Problem of the Day   ©Primary Concepts

Shoes at the Door

Word Problem

Mrs. Wordly insists that everyone take his or her shoes off by the front door so dirt doesn't get tracked into the house. There are three pairs of shoes by the front door now. The blue pair of shoes is *longer* than the white pair. The red pair of shoes is *shortest*.

Which pair of shoes is *longest*?

Talk About It

- Why are the shoes by the front door?
- Are your shoes longer or *shorter* than the person's shoes sitting next to you?
- Can the white pair of shoes be the longest? Explain.

Picture It   *Materials: paper and crayons or markers*

Draw the pairs of shoes by the front door. Compare the lengths.

Solution

The blue pair of shoes is the longest.

Sausages and Buns

Word Problem

Mr. Wordly decided to cook sausages for dinner. At the store, he got two packages of sausages. There were eight sausages in each package. Buns for the sausages came in packages of six. Mr. Wordly said to himself, "We have two buns already at home. How many packages of buns do I need to buy?" He got two packages of buns.

Are there *enough* buns for all the sausages?

Talk About It

- What is Mr. Wordly buying for dinner?
- Does Mr. Wordly already have some buns at home? (yes, two buns)
- How can we figure out how many sausages Mr. Wordly got?
- How can we figure out the total number of buns?

Use Symbols   *Materials: paper and pencil*

Use an oval to represent each sausage Mr. Wordly bought. Mark each sausage with an X to represent a bun. Are all the sausages marked?

Solution

There are *not enough* buns for all the sausages. Mr. Wordly has 16 sausages and only 14 buns.

The Heaviest Pumpkin

Word Problem

The neighbors had a pumpkin contest at Halloween to see who had grown the *heaviest* pumpkin. Three families entered their pumpkins, and all the pumpkins were going to be *weighed* on a large *scale*. The Wordlys' pumpkin was *heavier* than the Smiths' pumpkin. It was *lighter* than the Garcias' pumpkin.

Which family won the contest?

Talk About It

- Is the heaviest pumpkin always the biggest pumpkin?
- What is a scale?

Use Symbols   *Materials: paper and pencil*

Use letters to represent the families: *W* for the Wordlys, *S* for the Smiths, and *G* for the Garcias. Write the letters on paper in order from *lightest* to *heaviest*.

S W **G**

Solution

The Garcias won the contest. They had the heaviest pumpkin.

Performance Assessment

Word Problem

Mr. Wordly is making lunches for two Wordly children and four of their friends. He is making grilled cheese sandwiches for three children, a tuna sandwich for one child, and soup for two children.

How many slices of bread does he need?

Talk About It

- Are all the children having sandwiches?
- How many slices of bread does it take to make a sandwich? (two)

Solve It *Materials: paper and crayons or markers*

Use pictures and words to show your answer.

Solution

Mr. Wordly needs eight slices of bread.

Magazine Subscriptions

Word Problem

The oldest Wordly girl is selling subscriptions to magazines as a fund-raiser for her school. If she sells *more than* ten subscriptions, she earns a prize. On the *first* day, she sold four subscriptions. On the *second* day, she sold two subscriptions. Today is the *last* day to sell subscriptions.

How many subscriptions does she need to sell to get the prize?

Talk About It

- What is a magazine subscription? Does your family subscribe to any magazines?
- If the Wordly girl sells *exactly* ten subscriptions does she earn a prize? (no)
- What is the *fewest* number of subscriptions she can sell and still win a prize? (11)

Show It   *Materials: counters*

Use counters to represent each magazine subscription. Put out counters in one *row* for the subscriptions she has already sold. Then put out counters in another row for the subscriptions she still needs to sell. Make the total be 11 counters. Count the counters in the second row.

Solution

The Wordly girl must sell *at least* five subscriptions to win a prize.

The Party of 14

Word Problem

The oldest Wordly boy works at a restaurant. One night, a group of 14 people came to the restaurant. "We want to eat at one table," they said. Tables at the restaurant are *square*, and they seat one person on each *side*. Only four people can sit at each table. The Wordly boy knew what to do. "I'll put tables end to end," he decided.

How many tables does the Wordly boy need for the party?

Talk About It

- How many people need to be seated together? (14)
- Why do you think they want to sit altogether at one table?
- Have you ever been to a restaurant where tables were put together for a large group?

Picture It   *Materials: paper and pencil*

Draw square tables and chairs. Show the arrangement that will be needed for the party of 14 people.

Solution

The Wordly boy needs 6 tables for the party of 14 people.

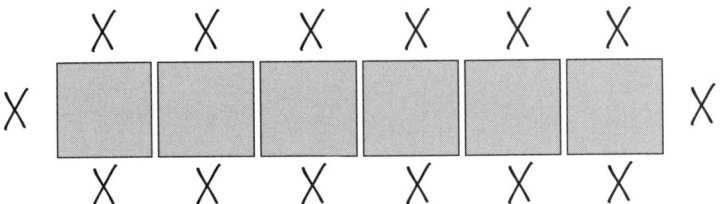

Word Problem of the Day   ©Primary Concepts

Coins in the Couch

Word Problem

When the youngest Wordly girl took the cushions off the couch to make a fort, she found a *nickel*, a *dime*, and six *pennies*. She ran to her mom and asked, "Mom, can I trade you these *coins* for a *quarter*?"

Was this a *fair trade*?

Talk About It

- How much is a nickel worth? a dime?
- How many pennies is a fair trade for a quarter? (25)

Show It   *Materials: play money—coins*

Show the coins the Wordly girl found in the couch. Use pennies to show an equal trade for the nickel. Show an equal trade for the dime. Count all the pennies.

Solution

It was not a fair trade. The Wordly girl had only 21 *cents*, and a quarter is worth 25 cents.

Game Time

Word Problem

When it is soccer season, the Wordlys' neighbors are busy running from one soccer game to another. One Saturday, their neighbors had soccer games at 9, 10, 11, and 12! Kevin's game was *earliest*. Rita's game was *latest*. Cooper's game was *later* than Elsie's game.

Whose game was at 11 *o'clock*?

Talk About It

- How many games are there? (four)
- What time is the earliest game? the latest game?
- If Cooper's game was later than Elsie's, did it happen *before* or *after* Elsie's game? (after)

Make a List   Materials: paper and pencil

Write the times of the games. Next to each time write the name of the person whose game it is.

Solution

Cooper's game was at 11:00 o'clock.

```
9 o'clock    Kevin
10 o'clock   Elsie
11 o'clock   Cooper
12 o'clock   Rita
```

Treats on a Hot Day

Word Problem

One very hot day, Mr. Wordly decided to run to the store and buy a package of eight frozen fruit bars as a treat. When he got home, he found five Wordly children, Mrs. Wordly, and Uncle Jim sitting on the back steps waiting for him. "I bought just *enough* fruit bars so all of us can have one," said Mr. Wordly.

Did Mr. Wordly buy just enough fruit bars?

Talk About It

- How many people were waiting on the back step for Mr. Wordly? (seven)
- Does Mr. Wordly get a fruit bar, too? (yes)
- If there are just enough fruit bars, would any be left over?

Use Symbols   *Materials: paper and pencil*

Draw a rectangle to represent each frozen fruit bar. Mark an X on each rectangle for each person.

Solution

Yes, Mr. Wordly bought just enough frozen fruit bars. There were *none* left over.

Making Lunches

Word Problem

Mrs. Wordly makes lunches each day for all the Wordly children. To make it simple, Mrs. Wordly told the children that they can choose to have a roast beef, ham, or tuna sandwich. For fruit, they can have an apple or an orange. One of the Wordly children announced that he wanted a different *combination* each *day of the school week.*

Is it possible to have a different lunch combo each day of the school week?

Talk About It

- How many days are there in the school week? (five)
- What is one combination the Wordly children can have?
- How will we know whether there are enough lunch combinations to have a different one each day?

Make a List   Materials: paper and pencil

Make a list of all the combinations of sandwich and fruit the Wordly children can choose from. Then count how many combinations there are.

Solution

Yes, they could have a different combination each day. There are five school days and six possibilities:

beef + apple	ham + apple	tuna + apple
beef + orange	ham + orange	tuna + orange

Penny Trading

Word Problem

The youngest Wordly boy came home one day with lots of *pennies*. He counted them out excitedly, "14 pennies!" "Where did you get those pennies?" one of the older Wordly kids asked. The little boy said, "I had just two *coins*: a *nickel* and a *dime*. My friend Marlon gave me all these pennies for my two coins."

Was this a *fair trade*?

Talk About It

- How much is a nickel worth? a dime?
- Why do you think the little Wordly boy traded coins with Marlon?
- What doesn't the little Wordly boy understand about money?

Show It   *Materials: play money—coins*

Show an equal trade for a nickel. Show an equal trade for a dime. Count the pennies.

Solution

It was not a fair trade. The little Wordly boy should have gotten 15 pennies in trade for a nickel and a dime.

©Primary Concepts   Word Problem of the Day

Performance Assessment

Word Problem

On Monday, Wednesday, and Friday, Mr. Wordly takes the bus to and from work. He rides his bike on the other days. He needs a bus token for each bus trip.

How many bus tokens does Mr. Wordly use in a week?

Talk About It

- What ways does Mr. Wordly get to work? (bike and bus)
- How many days of the week does Mr. Wordly ride the bus?
- How many bus tokens does Mr. Wordly need each day he rides the bus? (two, one to work and one back home)

Solve It   *Materials: paper and crayons or markers*

Use pictures and words to show your answer.

Solution

Mr. Wordly uses six tokens in a week. He takes the bus three days a week, once on the way to work and once back home.

Picture Day

Word Problem

It is picture day for the soccer team. There are 12 players on the team. The coach told them to stand in 3 *rows*.

How many players should be in each row?

Talk About It

- Have you ever played on a soccer team? What happens on picture day?
- What information do we know? (12 kids on the team, 3 rows)
- How could we figure out how many players to put in each row?

Show It   *Materials: counters*

Use counters to represent the players. Put the counters into three rows, with the same number of counters in each row. Count the number of counters in a row.

Solution

There should be four players in each row.

Stepping Stones

Word Problem

For Father's Day, the youngest Wordly children were making Mr. Wordly a mosaic stepping stone. The mosaic tiles came in three shapes: *triangle*, *square*, and *rectangle*. The children discovered that they could use two triangles to form a square and they could use two squares to form a large rectangle.

How many triangles would it take to form a large rectangle?

Talk About It

- Who knows what a mosaic is?
- How many *sides* does a triangle have? (three)
- What is the difference between a square and a rectangle?

Make a Model
Materials: triangles, squares (the size of two triangles), and rectangles (the size of two squares)

Use the triangles to make squares. Use the squares formed with triangles to make a rectangle. Count the number of triangles.

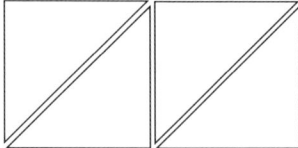

Solution

It takes four triangles to make a large rectangle.

Money in the Bank

Word Problem

The Wordly parents tell their children, "When you are old enough to get an allowance, you are old enough to save money." So they made this rule: *Half* of the money must go in the bank to save. The other half can be spent. For their allowance, the Wordly children get the number of *dollars* equal to their age.

How many dollars of her allowance should the 12-year-old Wordly put in the bank?

Talk About It

- What is an allowance? Do you get an allowance?
- How much allowance does the 12-year-old Wordly get? ($12)
- What does *half* mean?

Show It   *Materials: paper, scissors or play money—dollars*

Cut up paper to represent dollar bills, or use play money. Then divide $12 into two *even* amounts: one for saving and one for spending.

Solution

The 12-year-old Wordly should put $6 in the bank.

The Neighbor's Address

Word Problem

Mrs. Wordly is sending a card to the neighbors who live four doors down the street from the Wordlys. "I don't know their address, but I think it must be 10 Lilac Drive. We live at 2 Lilac Drive. Our next door neighbor is 4 Lilac Drive. The next house is 6 Lilac Drive. Two more houses down must be 10 Lilac Drive."

Is Mrs. Wordly right?

Talk About It

- What makes Mrs. Wordly think that the house number is 10?
- What do you notice about the numbers on the street?
- What are *even numbers*? What are *odd numbers*?
- Is there a *pattern* to the numbers on your street?
- What does *four doors down* mean? Which house is two doors down?

Find a Pattern   *Materials: paper and pencil*

Write the numbers in order. What do you notice? What numbers come next in the pattern?

#2   #4   #6   #____   #____

Solution

Yes, the next house would be #8, and the next house would be #10. The pattern is every other number (the even numbers).

Buying a Cat Door

Word Problem

The Wordlys decided to put in a cat door. The model they want to buy comes in three sizes: *small* for pets up to 12 *pounds, medium* for pets 12 to 40 pounds, and *large* for pets 40 to 80 pounds. The *striped* cat weighs 10 pounds, the *spotted* cat weighs 8 pounds, and the gray cat weighs 15 pounds. They want to get the *smallest* door possible.

Which size pet door should they buy?

Talk About It

- What is a cat door? Have you seen one before?
- Is it important to know which cat is the *lightest*? Explain.
- Are we looking for the *largest* door? Explain.

Use Symbols   *Materials: paper and pencil*

Draw three different-size boxes to represent the three different pet doors. Above the smallest box, write "up to 12." Above the medium-size box, write "12 to 40." Above the largest box, write "40 to 80." Now mark an X inside each box to represent the smallest door each Wordly cat could fit through. Which door is best for all three cats?

Solution

The Wordlys should buy the medium-size door.

A Gift for Grandma

Word Problem

One of the Wordly girls wants to make a special gift for her grandmother: a quilted pillowcase. The pillowcase will be made of *squares* of two different colors of soft fabric in a checkerboard design. The colors will be her grandma's favorites: pink and yellow. There will be three *rows* of squares. Each row will have six squares. *Every other* square will be a different color.

How many squares does the Wordly girl need of each color?

Talk About It

- What does a checkerboard look like? How will the pillowcase have a checkerboard design?
- Have you ever made a quilt? What did it look like? What was it made of?
- What is fabric?

Make a Model   Materials: small squares in two colors

Use the squares to make a model of the pillowcase the Wordly girl is planning to make.

Solution

The Wordly girl needs 9 squares of each color (18 squares in all).

Waitress Outfits

Word Problem

The oldest Wordly girl has a new job as a waitress at the Tricolor Restaurant. All the waitresses wear uniforms. She was given two pairs of pants: one red and one green. She was also given three shirts: one red, one green, and one white. "I want to look different each day," announced the girl.

How many different outfits can the Wordly girl wear?

Talk About It

- How many different pieces of clothing was the Wordly girl given for her uniform? (five) Is that what we are trying to find out? (no)
- What is the problem we are trying to solve?
- What is one outfit the girl could wear?

Picture It   *Materials: paper and crayons or markers*

Draw a picture of each different outfit the girl can wear. Count the number of outfits.

Solution

The Wordly girl can wear six different outfits: a white shirt and red pants, a white shirt and green pants, a red shirt and red pants, a red shirt and green pants, a green shirt and red pants, and a green shirt and green pants.

Performance Assessment

Word Problem

The middle Wordly girl is on a basketball team with nine other girls. At the first practice, the girls got to pick their jersey numbers. The numbers for the jerseys start at 5 and increase by two each time. There was one jersey for each girl. The Wordly girl chose the greatest number.

What was the Wordly girl's jersey number?

Talk About It

- What is a jersey? Why are there numbers on the jerseys?
- How many girls are on the basketball team? (ten)
- Can someone pick a jersey with the number 4 on it? (no, 4 is less than 5)
- Can someone pick a jersey with the number 6 on it? (no, the numbers increase by two so they are all odd)

Solve It   *Materials: paper and crayons or markers*

Use pictures and words to show your answer.

Solution

The Wordly girl's jersey number was 23.

Vocabulary Index

size (pp. 10, 27, 28, 30, 32, 35, 37, 55, 57, 64, 67, 69, 85)
vocabulary: small, smaller, smallest, medium, large, largest, big, bigger, biggest, shorter, shortest, tall, taller, tallest, longer, longest

shape (pp. 13, 18, 37, 60, 74, 82, 86)
vocabulary: circle, rectangle, square, triangle, side, shape, diagonal

sequence (pp. 3, 5, 6, 11, 25, 39, 53, 68, 73, 76)
vocabulary: first, second, third, fourth, eighth, last, next, before, after

direction (pp. 29, 39, 55)
vocabulary: backward, forward, left, right

amount (pp. 4, 12, 15, 16, 17, 23, 25, 31, 33, 34, 37, 45, 46, 47, 49, 56, 58, 64, 70, 73, 77, 83)
vocabulary: enough, not enough, more than, less than, too many, half, both

location (pp. 6, 11, 14, 18, 23, 30, 39, 43, 44, 55, 60, 65, 67, 73, 81, 86)
vocabulary: bottom, middle, top, closer, closest, farther, farthest, edge, halfway, inside, outside, above, below, between, center, front, column, row

equality (pp. 7, 19, 22, 23, 24, 26, 56, 57, 63, 65, 75, 79, 83)
vocabulary: equal, even, share, same, fair trade

money (pp. 2, 15, 28, 47, 57, 64, 75, 79, 83)
vocabulary: penny, nickel, dime, quarter, half dollar, dollar, silver, coins, cents, cost

time (pp. 21, 25, 36, 38, 42, 66, 76, 78, 80)
vocabulary: earlier, earliest, later, latest, days of the week, Sunday, Monday, Tuesday, Wednesday, Thursday, Friday, Saturday, calendar, o'clock, week

number (pp. 4, 6, 7, 22, 30, 34, 36, 40, 44, 46, 50, 51, 52, 55, 73, 77, 84, 88)
vocabulary: dozen, pair, twins, fewer, fewest, more, most, at least, none, zero, even numbers, odd numbers, exactly

logic (pp. 12, 34, 61, 62, 78)
vocabulary: either, or, combination

design (pp. 10, 23, 52, 53, 60, 68, 84, 85, 86)
vocabulary: plain, spotted, striped, pattern, every other

measurement (pp. 35, 54, 71, 85)
vocabulary: ruler, inches, thermometer, temperature, degree, colder, hotter, scale, weigh, heavier, heaviest, lighter, lightest, pound

©Primary Concepts   Word Problem of the Day

Strategies Index

Strategy	Pages
Act It Out	7, 11, 19, 29, 34, 55, 67
Do It	3, 13, 25, 42, 54, 66
Find a Pattern	53, 60, 68, 84
Make a List	5, 17, 21, 30, 31, 38, 62, 76, 78
Make a Model	37, 82, 86
Picture It	1, 6, 10, 14, 18, 23, 26, 33, 39, 41, 43, 45, 49, 52, 58, 69, 74, 87
Show It	2, 15, 22, 28, 35, 44, 47, 50, 57, 63, 65, 73, 75, 79, 81, 83
Use Symbols	4, 9, 12, 20, 27, 36, 46, 51, 59, 61, 70, 71, 77, 85